For permission requests, write to the publisher at the address below: Time For You Ltd

Plantation House, 19 Standing Stones,

Great Billing, Northampton NN3 9HA, United Kingdom

www.tiime4youfranchise.com

I0490295

"Time For You" is a registered trademark of Time For You Ltd. Printed in the United Kingdom.

Publisher: Independent Publishing Network. Publication date: 01/11/2024

ISBN: 978-1-83654-408-1

Author: Sam Stawarz

Please direct all enquiries to the author.

"Starting your own business is risky. Buying a franchise removes much of the risk – if you get the right franchise. That's where this book is essential. Sam has leveraged his extensive franchising experience to craft a comprehensive and insightful guide. Get this book and keep

it close as you embark on your business journey. Sam will help you determine if franchising is truly for you and guide you in avoiding common mistakes. Ten out of ten."

Greg Simpson, PR Expert, Press For Attention

www.pressforattention.com

"Sam has transformed his years of franchising knowledge into an easy-to-understand, powerful guide. Franchising is a less risky way to start your own business, and in this book, Sam further mitigates that risk. If you're even slightly interested in buying a franchise, you must read this book before investing a single penny."

Elliott Botterill, Digital Growth Specialist, BOTTERS. Digital Growth Agency

www.botters.co.uk

"Sam's book is an invaluable starting point for anyone considering a franchise. As a successful franchisor, Sam adopts a no-nonsense

approach to franchising. He highlights the advantages of franchising when done correctly while also warning potential franchisees of the pitfalls. All in all, it is a must-read for prospective franchisees."

Freddie Rayner, Franchise Founder and Author, Time For You,

www.time4youfranchise.com

About The Author

Sam Stawarz has been a pivotal figure in the franchising industry for over 14 years.

As an award-winning franchisor and the Managing Director at Time For You, a multi-million-pound franchise, Sam oversees a vast network of hundreds of franchisees.

His leadership and innovative approach have been instrumental in modernising the franchising landscape through the integration of cutting-edge technology, robust systems, and comprehensive training programmes.

Sam's dedication to growth and development has not only propelled Time For You to new heights but has also empowered countless businesses to flourish under his guidance.

Before We Start

Are you like I was 15 years ago?

Feeling trapped in the 9-to-5 grind, hoping for a life where your hard work directly benefits you and your family, rather than just being another cog in the corporate machine?

You're not alone. I've written this book, "The 7 Dirty Secrets of Franchising," for the frustrated middle class, the ambitious freelancers, and the determined entrepreneurs ready to take the leap into entrepreneurship through franchising. It's for those of us who have reached a career block or are feeling the weight of our job's demands, seeking not just a change, but a transformation. Let's embark on this journey together, where the value of our efforts is truly reflected in our achievements.

In my quest for work-life balance, I understand the desire for financial independence and the need to be part of a supportive business community. I've been where you are wanting to break free from the constraints of traditional employment and explore new avenues where passion and hard work can truly shine. But as we step into the world of franchising, it's crucial to uncover the hidden truths that could impact our journey.

Franchising is a fantastic way to get into business, but as with all opportunities it must come with a warning. This book exposes the seven dirty secrets of franchising, shedding light on the often undisclosed aspects of this industry. Even within a legally regulated business environment, not everything is voluntarily disclosed, leaving potential franchisees vulnerable. It's vital to equip yourself with the right questions to ask, ensuring you have a clear understanding of what you're stepping into.

My focus includes really frustrated employees, small business owners, side hustlers, and those involved in multi- level marketing (MLM) who are considering franchising as a viable path to success. You might be at a crossroads in your career, feeling overwhelmed by the demands of your current role, or perhaps you're just tired of the status quo. This book is my way of sharing practical insights and actionable strategies that will help you navigate the world of franchising and propel you toward tangible career progression, while also protecting yourself from potential pitfalls.

I believe in the power of franchising as a business opportunity, it's helped me and my family personally and I have seen it change the lives of many more. It's not just about making a change; it's about creating a life where our efforts lead to real, measurable success. However, it's imperative to gather all the necessary information about a franchise before making any commitments. You need to be aware of all the details to protect yourself from individuals who might view you merely as a 'cash cow' - an opportunity to further their ambitions at your expense.

In the bustling world of franchising, I've carved a niche that's as much about personal growth as it is about business development. As an award-winning entrepreneur who has weathered the storms of market downturns and emerged stronger, I bring a blend of resilience and optimism to the table. My philosophy is simple: empower individuals to become architects of their own destiny through the power of franchising. With over two decades of experience and having mentored hundreds to franchise success, I am committed to guiding you towards a future where financial independence and career satisfaction are not just dreams, but attainable realities.

As the author of this book, I want you to know that my journey in the franchise industry has been both challenging and rewarding. I've established myself as a trusted authority in franchise business development, not just through accolades and awards, but through a personal touch that sets me apart. My approach to franchising is unique; it's about fostering long-term relationships and maintaining an optimistic outlook even in the face of adversity.

Throughout my career, I have had the privilege of mentoring hundreds of individuals, helping them transform their careers and lives through franchising. My track record speaks for itself - I've successfully steered clients towards financial independence and career satisfaction, guiding them to become their own bosses and achieve their entrepreneurial dreams. But to get there, one must navigate the legal landscape carefully, understanding that employment law does not apply to franchise agreements.

In the heart of every frustrated employee lies a dream that's been deferred; the dream of a life where work serves as a joyful pursuit rather than a burdensome chore. I see you, the hard-working individual who's been giving their all, yet feeling like you're running on a treadmill that's going nowhere. This book is my response to your silent plea for a career that aligns with your values, for a life where your work amplifies your happiness rather than detracts from it. If left unaddressed, the path you're on can lead to more than just career dissatisfaction; it can erode the very fabric of your well-being. It's time to take control, and I'm here to guide you towards a brighter future where your professional life is a source of fulfilment and joy.

I understand the struggle of juggling work commitments with personal life, the constant push and pull that leaves you yearning for a change. Many of us find ourselves stuck in jobs that no longer bring satisfaction, trapped in routines that drain rather than energise us. This frustration, coupled with the aspiration for financial independence and a better career, is a powerful motivator that drives me to write this book. By equipping yourself with the right information, you can confidently navigate the franchising landscape and choose the path that best suits your aspirations.

In the pages that follow, I'll try to demystify the world of franchising. You'll learn not just to choose a franchise, but to choose a future - one that resonates with your deepest aspirations for growth, family, and fulfilment. This book isn't just about making a business decision; it's about crafting the life you've always wanted, with the blueprint of franchising as your guide.

By delving into this book, you'll gain a comprehensive understanding of the franchise business model and its immense potential for personal and professional growth. You'll learn to navigate the franchising landscape with an optimistic yet realistic approach, equipping yourself to avoid common pitfalls that many encounter. Remember, the key to safeguarding your interests lies in asking the right questions.

By doing so, you can uncover the hidden secrets of franchising and make an informed decision.

This journey will arm you with the tools needed to critically evaluate franchise opportunities, ensuring they align with your personal values and long-term goals. You'll discover strategies for achieving work-life balance through the franchise model, leading to greater overall satisfaction and a more harmonious life.

We'll also delve into the business process that has not only proven successful for myself but for countless others who have taken the leap into franchising. We'll start by laying a rock-solid foundation, ensuring that every step you take is on stable ground, ready to bear the weight of your ambitions.

From there, we'll harness the demand in your unique market, optimise every cog in your operational machine, and continuously refine our approach based on real- world feedback. This isn't just about starting a business; it's about nurturing it, watching it grow, and reaping the rewards of your determination and hard work.

The HUGE Benefits Of Franchising

In today's rapidly shifting economic landscape, the concept of job security has become almost mythical.

Once upon a time, the dream of a stable job, a secure pension, and a comfortable retirement after decades of dedication to a single employer seemed attainable.

However, this dream has been shattered by waves of corporate restructuring, economic downturns, and, most recently, the global pandemic. These changes have left many individuals questioning the reliability of traditional employment and searching for alternative paths to financial stability and personal fulfilment.

With all this uncertainty, franchising emerges as a brilliant opportunity. For those disillusioned with the unpredictability of the corporate world, franchising offers a compelling alternative: the chance to become your own boss while benefiting from the support and recognition of an established brand. The journey from employee to entrepreneur is not without its challenges, but with the right franchise, it can be a rewarding venture.

Why Choose Franchising?

Franchising presents a unique business model that combines the autonomy of entrepreneurship with the security of a proven business strategy. Unlike starting a business from scratch, where the path is fraught with unknowns and potential pitfalls, franchising provides a road map crafted from the franchisor's experience and expertise. This model reduces the risks associated with new ventures and offers a structured environment in which to thrive.

The diversity within the franchising world is vast. Today, franchising extends far beyond the fast-food industry, encompassing sectors as varied as healthcare, education, fitness, and home services. With hundreds of franchise options available, aspiring entrepreneurs are likely to find a franchise that aligns with their passions and goals. Whether you're interested in providing essential services or indulging a personal interest, there's a franchise opportunity waiting for you.

One of the most significant advantages of choosing a franchise is the groundwork that has already been laid by the franchisor. This includes detailed market research, customer analysis, and financial planning. As a franchisee, you inherit a wealth of knowledge that would take years to accumulate independently.

This comprehensive support system not only simplifies the process of starting a business but also increases the likelihood of success.

The Power of Optimism

Coming from a catering background, where shouting at people to get things done was part of the job, I found myself in a high-pressure and (very) underpaid world.

However, franchising opened a new path for me, away from the relentless demands of catering.

Just as I entered the catering industry with a passion for food and an optimistic view of my future, I approached franchising with the same mindset. I wasn't entirely sure if I was cut out for business, but I knew I wanted to change.

In this journey, optimism became my superpower.

Optimism allowed me to see beyond the immediate challenges and focus on the potential for growth and success. It provided the resilience needed to navigate the ups and downs of entrepreneurship. By maintaining a positive outlook, I could embrace opportunities and learn from setbacks, ultimately leading to a fulfilling and prosperous career in franchising.

The franchising industry has shown remarkable resilience and growth, even amidst economic uncertainties.

As traditional employment landscapes shift, franchising offers a stable alternative for aspiring entrepreneurs.

Here are some key insights into the current state of the franchise market:

1.   Diverse Opportunities

Franchising extends beyond the fast-food sector, encompassing industries such as healthcare, education, fitness, and home services. This diversity allows entrepreneurs to find opportunities that align with their interests and skills.

2.   Economic Impact

The franchise industry contributes significantly to the economy, providing numerous jobs and stimulating local markets. It offers a structured business model that reduces the risks associated with starting a business from scratch.

3.   Growth Trends

Despite global economic challenges, the franchise sector continues to expand. This growth is driven by the increasing demand for services and the appeal of a proven business model that offers both autonomy and support.

4.   Investment Appeal

Franchising is attractive to investors due to its established brand recognition and comprehensive support systems.

This reduces the time and effort required to build a business reputation, leading to quicker market penetration and profitability.

5.   Future Outlook

As more individuals seek financial independence and control over their professional lives, the franchise model is likely to grow in popularity. Ongoing innovations and adaptations in response to market demands will continue to drive the industry forward.

For those considering entering the franchise market, thorough research and engagement with franchise consultants can provide valuable guidance. Understanding current trends and the competitive landscape is crucial for making informed decisions and achieving long-term success.

Source: https://www.franchisedirect.com/information/industry-statistics

Why Choose Franchising?

Franchising offers two primary benefits that set it apart from independent business ventures: proper training and support, and the power of a recognised brand.

Unparalleled Training and Support

The success of a franchisee directly impacts the franchisor, creating a vested interest in ensuring that franchisees are well-equipped to succeed. Good franchisors provide extensive training programmes designed to impart the skills and knowledge necessary to operate the business effectively. This training covers everything from day-to-day operations to advanced sales techniques and customer service excellence.

Moreover, the support doesn't end once the business is up and running. Good franchisors offer ongoing assistance to help franchisees navigate challenges and seize opportunities. This continuous support is a cornerstone of the franchising model, providing peace of mind and a safety net for those new to entrepreneurship.

A Known Brand

In the world of business, brand recognition is invaluable. Starting a business with an established brand means that you are not building a reputation from scratch. Customers are already familiar with the brand, which can lead to quicker market penetration and increased trust. This recognition can significantly ease the path to profitability and growth, as customers are more likely to engage with a brand they know and trust.

Who Thrives in Franchising?

While franchising offers numerous advantages, it is not a one-size-fits-all solution. Success in franchising requires certain qualities and commitments. Prospective franchisees should possess a willingness to learn and be coached, as well as the financial stability to support the initial investment and ongoing costs. A strong work ethic and a genuine passion for the business are also crucial. Those who thrive in franchising are often individuals who are eager to take control of their professional lives while adhering to a proven system.

Understanding Franchise Models

Franchising offers a variety of business models, each with its unique operational structure, benefits, and challenges. Understanding these models is crucial for aspiring franchisees to make informed decisions.

Here's an overview of the key aspects of franchise models.

Types of Franchise Models:

- Product Distribution Franchises: Focus on the supply of products, where the franchisee sells the franchisor's products.

Examples include automobile dealerships and soft drink distributors.

•   Business Format Franchises: Provide a complete business system, including the brand, products, and operational procedures. Fast-food chains and retail stores often use this model.

•   Management Franchises: In this model, franchisees manage a business or service, such as a cleaning service or recruitment agency, without being directly involved in the day-to-day operations.

Benefits and Challenges:

•   Product Distribution Franchises: Benefit from established brand recognition but may face challenges with inventory management and competition.

•   Business Format Franchises: Offer comprehensive support and a proven business model but can involve higher initial costs and ongoing fees.

•   Management Franchises: Provide flexibility and scalability but require strong leadership and management skills.

Latest Trends in Franchising:

- Sustainability and Eco-Friendly Practices: Consumers are increasingly favouring businesses that prioritise sustainability, prompting franchises to adopt eco- friendly practices.

- Health and Wellness: The demand for health-conscious products and services is growing, leading to a rise in franchises focused on fitness, nutrition, and wellness.

- Customisation and Personalisation: Franchises are offering more personalised experiences to meet consumer preferences, enhancing customer engagement and loyalty.

Impact of Technology:

- Technology is revolutionising franchising by streamlining operations, enhancing customer experiences, and providing data-driven insights. From mobile apps to advanced POS systems, technology is shaping the future of the industry by increasing efficiency and connectivity.

Real-World Examples:

- McDonald's: A classic example of a business format franchise, McDonald's success lies in its consistent brand experience and operational efficiency.

- 7-Eleven: Known for its adaptability, 7-Eleven has successfully expanded globally by tailoring its product offerings to local markets.

- Time For You Domestic Cleaning: A management franchise model that excels in providing consistent, high-quality cleaning services through a well-structured support system.

These examples highlight the importance of a robust operational framework, adaptability to market demands, and the strategic use of technology in achieving franchise success.

Top Franchising Sectors

The franchising industry is vast and diverse, offering opportunities across multiple sectors.

Here are some of the top franchising sectors that have shown significant growth and promise:

Food and Beverage:

Quick-Service Restaurants (QSRs): This sector remains a dominant force in franchising, with brands like McDonald's, Subway, and Starbucks leading the way. The appeal lies in the consistent demand for convenient dining options.

Fast Casual and Speciality Foods: Growing consumer interest in healthier and more diverse food options has fuelled the growth of fast-casual dining and speciality food franchises.

Health and Wellness:

Fitness Centres: With an increasing focus on health, fitness franchises such as Anytime Fitness and Orangetheory Fitness are thriving.

Health Services: Franchises offering services like physical therapy, nutrition consulting, and senior care are gaining traction due to the ageing population and wellness trends.

Home Services:

Cleaning and Maintenance: As busy lifestyles prevail, franchises providing home cleaning, landscaping, and repair services continue to expand.

Home Improvement: Franchises offering renovation and home enhancement services cater to homeowners seeking to upgrade their living spaces.

Education and Childcare:

Tutoring and Learning Centres: With the increasing emphasis on education, franchises like Kumon and Tutor Doctor are popular choices for parents seeking supplemental education for their children.

Childcare Services: The demand for quality childcare facilities has led to the growth of franchises such as The Goddard School and Primrose Schools.

Retail:

Speciality Retail: Franchises focusing on niche markets, from pet supplies to beauty products, are capitalising on consumer preferences for specialised shopping experiences.

Convenience Stores: Brands like 7-Eleven and Circle K continue to thrive due to their strategic locations and diverse product offerings.

Technology and Business Services:

IT Support and Digital Marketing: As businesses increasingly rely on technology, franchises offering IT support and digital marketing services are in high demand.

Business Consulting: Franchises providing business advisory and consulting services cater to entrepreneurs and small businesses seeking expertise.

These sectors highlight the adaptability and innovation within the franchising industry, offering a range of opportunities for potential franchisees to explore. Whether driven by consumer trends or technological advancements, these top sectors demonstrate the dynamic nature of franchising and its ability to meet diverse market needs.

Source: https://www.franchise.org

Key Success Factors in Franchising

Success in franchising is multi-faceted, requiring a blend of strategic planning, effective management, and strong relationships.

Here are the key factors that contribute to thriving in the franchising world:

• Understanding the Franchise Model: Grasping the intricacies of the franchise model is essential. This includes knowing the legal, operational, and financial aspects that define the franchise relationship.

• Comprehensive Market Research: Conducting thorough market research helps identify consumer needs, competitive landscape, and potential growth opportunities, providing a solid foundation for decision- making.

• Robust Business Plan: A well-structured business plan outlines the path to success, detailing goals, strategies, and financial projections. It serves as a roadmap for the franchisee's journey.

• Financial Management and Capital Reserves: Sound financial management ensures the business remains sustainable, with adequate capital reserves to weather unforeseen challenges.

- Strong Leadership and Management Skills: Effective leadership is crucial for guiding the franchise team, fostering a positive work environment, and ensuring operational efficiency.

- Effective Marketing and Branding Strategies: Leveraging effective marketing and branding strategies helps attract and retain customers, reinforcing the franchise's market position.

- Commitment to the Franchise System: Adhering to the franchisor's established systems and processes ensures consistency and quality, which are vital for brand reputation.

- Building a Good Relationship with the Franchisor: A strong, communicative relationship with the franchisor facilitates support, guidance, and mutual growth.

- Ongoing Training and Support: Continuous training and support from the franchisor empower franchisees to stay updated with industry trends and operational improvements.

- Adaptability and Continuous Improvement: Successful franchisees are adaptable, embracing change and seeking continuous improvement to meet evolving market demands.

- Customer Service Excellence: Providing exceptional customer service builds loyalty and enhances the franchise's reputation, driving repeat business.

- Compliance with Franchise Agreements: Adhering to the terms of the franchise agreement ensures legal compliance and maintains a harmonious relationship with the franchisor.

- Networking with Other Franchisees: Engaging with other franchisees offers valuable insights, shared experiences, and collaborative opportunities.

- Leveraging Technology for Efficiency: Utilising technology enhances operational efficiency, streamlines processes, and improves customer interactions.

- Exit Strategy Planning: Having a well-defined exit strategy ensures a smooth transition when the time comes to sell or transfer the franchise.

Taking the next steps into franchising

For those considering franchising, the first step is to determine whether this path aligns with their personal and professional aspirations.

Engaging with a franchise consultant can be an invaluable part of this process. These professionals specialise in matching individuals with franchise opportunities that suit their skills, interests, and financial capabilities. Their expertise can guide you toward a franchise that not only meets your needs but also sets you on a path to success.

Franchising represents a powerful vehicle for achieving entrepreneurial dreams. By leveraging the support of an established brand and the insights of industry experts, aspiring business owners can embark on a journey that combines independence with the security of a tested business model.

As you explore the world of franchising, remember that the key to success lies in thorough research, careful consideration, and a clear understanding of the franchise agreement. With the right preparation, franchising can lead to a fulfilling and prosperous future.

In conclusion, the world of franchising offers a compelling alternative to traditional employment, providing a structured environment for entrepreneurial success.

Whether you're driven by the desire for financial independence, the pursuit of a passion, or the dream of owning your own business, franchising can be the key to unlocking your potential.

Embrace the opportunity, and take the first step toward a new and exciting chapter in your professional life.

The Seven DIRTY secrets of franchising revealed!

Protect yourself from franchise risk by finding out about the DIRTY secrets franchisors use to get you to sign up to their franchise.

Exposing the Seven DIRTY Secrets of franchising?

Protect yourself from franchise risk by finding out about the DIRTY secrets franchisors use to get you to sign up to their franchise.

Franchising is a popular business model in the UK, offering many individuals the opportunity to step into entrepreneurship with a safety net of support and a proven business concept. However, while the majority of UK franchises operate with integrity and transparency, it's essential to acknowledge that not every franchise will be the perfect fit for every aspiring entrepreneur.

Understanding the nuances of franchising can help you make an informed decision about whether this path aligns with your personal and professional goals.

Understanding Franchising: A Path to a Better Life? Or A Risk You Should Avoid?

If you're reading this, you might be seeking a better work/ life balance, a new career path, or simply the fulfilment that comes with owning your own business. Franchising offers a unique opportunity to achieve these goals, providing a structured way to own and operate a business with the backing of an established franchise. The appeal of franchising lies in its ability to offer a relatively lower- risk entry into business ownership, as franchisees benefit from the franchisor's experience, brand recognition, and operational support.

However, despite the advantages, it's crucial to approach franchising with a clear understanding of what it entails.

While extensive information is available about franchising, there are significant gaps and omissions in the general knowledge that prospective franchisees often encounter.

This report, crafted by a franchising insider, aims to shed light on these hidden aspects, ensuring you have a comprehensive understanding before making any commitments.

Why is it necessary to uncover these hidden franchising secrets?

The answer lies in the fact that, even within a legally regulated business environment, not everything is voluntarily disclosed. This lack of transparency can leave potential franchisees vulnerable, especially if they are not equipped with the right questions to ask. Even when information is disclosed, it may not always be entirely accurate or complete. Some franchisors, driven by selfish motives, might be tempted to withhold certain details or present them in a way that serves their interests more than yours.

It's important to emphasise that not all franchisors are unscrupulous. Many are genuinely committed to the success of their franchisees and operate with integrity. Franchising remains a viable and often successful way to enter the business world. There are hundreds of reputable franchises in the UK, each offering a unique opportunity to launch and sustain a business with the backing of an established brand.

However, the information that is legally hidden from you can have severe implications once you've committed financially and signed a franchise agreement. These agreements often bind you for several years, sometimes up to five or ten, making it crucial to fully understand the terms and conditions before signing.

The Legal Landscape of Franchising

As previously stated, one critical aspect to understand is that employment law does not apply to franchise agreements. As a franchisee, you are entering into a business contract, and not an employment contract. This distinction is significant because it means that if you are dissatisfied with the terms of the franchise agreement, you cannot rely on employment law protections to extricate yourself. Instead, any disputes would need to be resolved through civil law, which can be a complex and costly process.

Therefore, it's imperative to gather all the necessary information about a franchise before making any commitments. You need to be aware of all the details to protect yourself from individuals who might view you merely as a 'cash cow' - an opportunity to further their ambitions at your expense.

Protecting Yourself: The Power of the Right Questions

The key to safeguarding your interests lies in asking the right questions. By doing so, you can uncover the hidden secrets of franchising and make an informed decision.

Armed with this information, you have several options:

•   Proceed with the Deal as It Stands: If the franchise meets your expectations and aligns with your goals, you may choose to move forward with the agreement as it is.

•   Negotiate Custom Terms: If certain aspects of the franchise agreement don't suit you, consider negotiating changes that better align with your needs and objectives.

•   Walk Away: If the franchise doesn't meet your criteria or raises too many red flags, it's perfectly acceptable to walk away and retain your financial resources.

Remember, knowledge is power. By equipping yourself with the right information, you can confidently navigate the franchising landscape and choose the path that best suits your aspirations.

Always Make an Informed Decision

Franchising can be a rewarding and lucrative path to business ownership, but it's not without its challenges. By understanding the hidden aspects of franchising and asking the right questions, you can make an informed decision that aligns with your personal and professional goals.

Remember, the key to success in franchising lies in thorough research, careful consideration, and a clear understanding of the franchise agreement. With the right knowledge and preparation, you can embark on a franchising journey that leads to a fulfilling and prosperous future.

SECRET 1: The Franchise Contract Favours The Franchisor

The Franchise Contract: A Document Favouring the Franchisor

Franchise contracts are inherently designed to benefit the franchisor. This isn't necessarily a sign of malice but rather a standard practice to protect their business model and ensure consistency across franchises. However, this means that as a prospective franchisee, you must be vigilant.

The contract will likely be lengthy and filled with complex legal jargon. It's crucial to read every word before signing. The franchisor has spent considerable resources crafting this document to maintain control and safeguard their interests.

ALWAYS READ THE CONTRACT!

Understanding the contract is your first line of defence. While you should do your best to comprehend the terms, it's equally important to seek professional legal advice.

Don't cut corners here; investing in a solicitor who specialises in franchise law can save you from future headaches. Your local family lawyer might not have the necessary expertise, so look for legal professionals who have experience with franchise agreements. They can review the contract, highlight potential pitfalls, and suggest amendments, often for a fixed fee. It's wise to shop around and compare services.

Beyond legal advice, consider consulting an experienced businessperson who can provide a practical perspective on the contract. They might spot business-related concerns that a lawyer might overlook. This dual approach - legal and business - ensures you're making an informed decision before committing financially.

Don't Be Afraid To Ask Questions

The questions you ask before signing a franchise agreement can significantly impact your understanding and future success. By asking the right questions, you can uncover hidden details, clarify terms, and ensure that the agreement aligns with your expectations and goals.

Understanding the financial aspects is crucial. You need to inquire about initial and ongoing costs and be vigilant for any hidden fees that might not be immediately apparent. Operationally, it's vital to understand the support the franchisor offers, including how training is conducted and what resources are available to you. From a legal standpoint, clarifying the terms for termination or renewal, as well as any restrictions on selling the franchise, is essential.

When framing questions, aim to uncover hidden details by using open-ended questions that encourage detailed responses. Request examples or case studies to illustrate points, and be specific about areas of concern, such as marketing support or territory rights.

Questions play a pivotal role in negotiating a better franchise agreement. By identifying areas for negotiation, such as fees or support levels, you can ensure that any ambiguous terms are clarified to avoid future misunderstandings. It is also crucial to ensure that any verbal promises are documented in writing.

Consider the long-term implications of the franchise agreement by asking about growth opportunities within the franchise and how the franchisor plans to adapt to market changes. Understanding the exit options if the business doesn't perform as expected is also important.

To document answers and promises from the franchisor, take detailed notes during meetings and conversations. Request written confirmation of any commitments or changes to the agreement, and use email or other written communication to create a paper trail.

The impact of not asking the right questions can lead to unexpected challenges and dissatisfaction. You might find yourself locked into unfavourable terms or unprepared for the realities of running the franchise.

Reflecting on case studies can illustrate this point. In one success story, a franchisee who asked detailed questions about marketing support negotiated additional resources that significantly boosted their business. Conversely, a failure example involves a franchisee who didn't inquire about territory rights, only to face competition from another franchisee in their area.

Developing a questioning mindset is about becoming your own best advocate. Cultivating this mindset means being proactive, curious, and sceptical. By advocating for yourself, you can make informed decisions that align with your business goals. Remember, the more you know, the better prepared you'll be to succeed in the franchising world.

Making informed Decisions

When it comes to franchising, making informed decisions is paramount to ensuring a successful business venture. The cornerstone of this process is the thorough review of the franchise agreement. This document outlines the terms and conditions of your relationship with the franchisor and sets the foundation for your business operations. It's crucial to approach this review with diligence and a critical eye.

Identifying clauses that could be potentially unfavourable is an essential skill. Look out for terms that may limit your autonomy or impose excessive fees. Pay attention to clauses regarding termination, renewal, and transfer of the franchise, as these can significantly impact your long-term business prospects.

Negotiating terms within the franchise agreement is not only possible but advisable. Approach negotiations with a clear understanding of your needs and objectives. Be prepared to discuss aspects such as fees, support levels, and territory rights. Successful negotiation can lead to a more balanced agreement that better serves your interests.

The long-term implications of the franchisor-franchisee relationship cannot be overstated. This partnership will shape your business's future, so it's vital to understand how the franchisor's policies and practices will affect your operations. Consider how the franchisor plans to adapt to market changes and what support they will provide to foster your growth.

Real-life examples highlight how franchise agreements have historically favoured franchisors in disputes. These cases underscore the importance of understanding the agreement's terms and seeking modifications where necessary. Learning from these examples can help you avoid similar pitfalls.

Seeking legal advice on franchise agreements is a critical step in the decision-making process. A solicitor with expertise in franchise law can provide invaluable insights into the agreement's complexities. They can help you identify potential issues, suggest amendments, and ensure that your rights are protected.

Understanding your rights and obligations under the franchise agreement is fundamental to your success as a franchisee. Familiarise yourself with the duties you are expected to fulfil and the rights you are entitled to. This knowledge will empower you to operate confidently within the framework of the agreement and to address any issues that arise with clarity and assurance.

Bad Franchisors, Why do they do it?

In the world of franchising, not all franchisors operate with the best interests of their franchisees at heart.

Understanding the motivations and behaviours of less scrupulous franchisors can help prospective franchisees navigate potential pitfalls.

•   Profit Maximisation is often at the forefront for some franchisors, who prioritise their financial gain over the success of their franchisees. This focus on short- term profits can lead to decisions that undermine the long-term sustainability of the franchise network. Such franchisors might impose high fees or inadequate support structures, leaving franchisees struggling to maintain profitability.

•   Lack of Oversight A can also plague franchise systems. This often results from a franchisor's over extension, where rapid expansion leads to inadequate monitoring and support. In some cases, it may simply be a matter of disinterest in the day-to-day operations of individual franchisees. Without proper oversight, franchisees may find themselves without the guidance and resources needed to thrive.

•   Misaligned Objectives can create significant challenges within a franchise network. When franchisors and franchisees have differing goals, it can lead to conflicting strategies and priorities. For example, a franchisor focused on rapid expansion might push for aggressive sales targets, while franchisees are more concerned with sustainable growth and customer satisfaction.

• Inexperienced Leadership can be detrimental to a franchise system. Franchisors with insufficient experience in managing a network may make poor decisions that negatively affect their franchisees. These decisions can range from inadequate training programs to ineffective marketing strategies, leaving franchisees without the tools needed for success.

Finally, some franchisors engage in Exploitative Practices, leveraging their power to impose unfair terms and conditions on franchisees. This can include restrictive contracts, excessive fees, or unrealistic performance expectations. Exploitative franchisors may view franchisees merely as revenue streams, disregarding their success and well-being.

By recognising these potential issues, prospective franchisees can better assess the franchisors they consider partnering with, ensuring they choose a franchise system that values and supports its network for long-term success.

SECRET 2: Don't Rely On Verbal Agreements

The Importance Of Written Agreements

In the world of franchising, verbal promises can often be misleading. The excitement of starting a new business venture can sometimes cloud judgement, especially when a persuasive salesperson is involved. It's not uncommon for sales representatives to make enticing promises to close a deal, but it's crucial to remember that unless these promises are documented, they hold little legal weight.

Salespeople are trained to highlight the best aspects of a franchise, sometimes embellishing details to make the opportunity appear more attractive. They might promise high earnings, minimal effort, or guaranteed success. While these claims can be enticing, it's essential to approach them with caution. The adage "if it sounds too good to be true, it probably is" holds significant relevance here.

IF IT'S PROMISED VERBALLY IT'S NO GOOD. GET IT IN WRITING!

Franchisors, eager to expand their network, might downplay potential challenges or exaggerate the support you'll receive. It's your responsibility to sift through these promises critically. Always question the feasibility of claims made during the sales pitch.

For instance, if you're told that the franchise will guarantee a specific income within a short period, ask for evidence.

Request to see financial statements or speak to existing franchisees who can verify these claims.

The key to protecting yourself is to ensure all promises are documented in writing. If a franchisor makes a specific promise that is crucial to your decision-making, insist

that it be included in the franchise agreement or as an addendum. A written agreement signed and dated by both parties eliminates ambiguity and provides a clear reference point should any disputes arise in the future.

For example, if you're promised exclusive territory rights, ensure this is explicitly stated in the contract. If there are promises of marketing support or training, these should also be detailed with specifics about what is included and any associated costs.

Even with written agreements, it's vital to read and understand the fine print. Legal documents can be complex, and it's easy to overlook clauses that could impact you negatively. This is where professional legal advice becomes invaluable. A franchise solicitor can help you interpret the contract, ensuring that all verbal promises are accurately reflected and that there are no hidden clauses that could pose problems down the line.

Beyond getting promises in writing, conducting thorough due diligence is essential. Verify claims made by the franchisor by speaking with a diverse group of existing franchisees. Don't just rely on the ones suggested by the franchisor. Ask them about their experiences, challenges, and whether the promises made to them were fulfilled.

This firsthand insight can provide a more realistic picture of what to expect.

Visit franchise locations if possible. Seeing the business in action can reveal aspects that aren't apparent through conversations or documents. It gives you a sense of the day-to-day operations and whether the franchise aligns with your expectations and lifestyle.

So while verbal promises can be persuasive, they are not legally binding. Protect yourself by ensuring all important promises are documented in writing. This step, combined with diligent research and legal advice, empowers you to make informed decisions.

By approaching franchising with a critical eye and a focus on documentation, you can safeguard your investment and increase your chances of success in your new business venture.

Always Read The Contract

Sorry to have to re-visit this one so soon! But it's really important!

In the realm of franchising, the significance of written contracts cannot be overstated. They provide a firm foundation for the franchise relationship, clearly outlining the commitments and expectations of both parties.

Unfortunately, many franchisees fall into the trap of relying on verbal agreements, which can lead to significant pitfalls. Verbal promises often lack the legal enforceability of written contracts, leaving franchisees vulnerable to unmet expectations.

Written agreements carry the weight of legality, serving as a reliable reference in the event of disputes. They ensure that all promises are documented, reducing the risk of misunderstandings. To protect oneself, it is crucial to insist on having every important promise included in the contract. This includes specifics about earnings, support, and territory rights.

When reviewing a franchise contract, it's essential to be thorough. Carefully read each clause and seek clarification on any terms that are unclear. Engaging legal counsel

is invaluable in this process, as they can help interpret complex legal language and ensure that the contract aligns with your expectations. This step is crucial in preventing costly mistakes.

There are countless real-life examples of disputes arising from verbal agreements. These often revolve around unfulfilled promises, such as guaranteed income or exclusive territories not documented in writing. Such cases emphasise the necessity of having a written contract to avoid legal battles.

Negotiating contract terms requires preparation and a clear understanding of your needs. It's important to be assertive, seeking mutually beneficial terms. The long-term impact of contractual obligations on your business cannot be overlooked, as they dictate the operational framework and growth potential of the franchise.

Before signing, verify key contractual elements like territory rights, support provisions, and termination clauses. This checklist acts as a safeguard, ensuring that all critical aspects are addressed. By approaching franchising with a critical eye and focusing on documentation, you can safeguard your investment and increase your chances of success.

If it's too good to be true, it probably is!

In the world of franchising, the old adage "if it's too good to be true, it usually is" rings especially true. When entering a franchise agreement, it's essential to approach enticing promises with a healthy dose of scepticism. The excitement of a new venture can sometimes overshadow the need for caution, particularly when verbal promises are involved.

Relying on verbal promises in franchising can lead to significant pitfalls. These promises, often made in the heat of negotiations, may not hold up if not captured in writing. Without a written record, franchisees may find themselves without recourse if these promises go unfulfilled. This is why getting agreements in writing is crucial. A written contract provides a clear, legally enforceable record of the commitments made by both parties, reducing the risk of misunderstandings and disputes.

To ensure verbal agreements are captured in the franchise contract, it's important to insist on their inclusion during the drafting process. Every promise that is critical to your decision-making should be documented in the contract

or as an addendum. This includes specific terms about earnings, support, training, and territory rights. Having these details in writing eliminates ambiguity and provides a solid foundation for the franchise relationship.

Real-life examples abound of disputes caused by reliance on verbal agreements. These often involve promises of guaranteed income or exclusive territories that were not documented, leading to legal battles and financial losses. Such cases underscore the importance of thorough documentation and the risks of taking verbal promises at face value.

When negotiating and documenting important terms and conditions, preparation is key. Enter negotiations with a clear understanding of your priorities and be assertive in seeking terms that align with your business goals. It's also wise to engage legal counsel to review the contract, ensuring that all verbal promises are accurately reflected and that there are no hidden clauses that could pose problems later on.

By approaching franchising with a critical eye and a focus on documentation, you can protect your investment and increase your chances of success. Remember, if a deal sounds too good to be true, it probably is - so get it in writing.

Contractual Challenges

When I first ventured into the world of franchising, I quickly learned the hard way that the excitement of a new opportunity can sometimes cloud one's judgement. I remember sitting across from a franchise representative who painted a picture so rosy that it was hard not to get swept up in the dream.

Promises of high earnings and minimal effort were enticing, but I knew I had to ground myself in reality.

One of the first lessons I learned was the critical importance of legal advice in franchise agreements. I cannot stress enough how essential it is to consult with a solicitor who specialises in franchising. Their expertise can save you from potential pitfalls that aren't immediately obvious. During my journey, I made it a point to have every clause of the contract reviewed by my solicitor. It was an investment that paid off tenfold by providing peace of mind and clarity.

Negotiating contract terms was another eye-opener. It's easy to feel intimidated when facing a well-established franchisor, but remember, negotiation is part of the process. While you might not always succeed - especially when it comes to financial terms - it's worth the effort to try. I found that being prepared and knowing exactly what I wanted helped me negotiate terms that were more favourable than I initially expected.

I also developed what I like to call the "Franchisee's Checklist for Contractual Agreements." This became my go-to guide, ensuring that I double-checked all promises, terms, fees, and other critical details. Having this checklist was invaluable in keeping me organised and focused during the review process.

Understanding the fine print is where many franchisees stumble. Legal documents can be dense and full of jargon, making it easy to overlook important details. I learned to lean on my solicitor for this, but also took the time to do my own research and, when necessary, ask the franchisor for clarification. This proactive approach helped me feel more confident and informed about the commitments I was making.

Reflecting on these experiences, I can't emphasise enough the importance of being diligent and thorough when entering a franchise agreement. It's a significant step that can shape your business future, so take the time to ensure everything is in order.

Trust me, it's worth it.

SECRET 3: The 'Pet List' of Franchisees

Why would they give you a 'pet list'?

When considering investing in a franchise, one of the most valuable resources available is the insight and experiences of current franchisees. Franchisors often provide a list of franchisees you can contact, commonly referred to as the 'pet list.' However, it's crucial to understand the potential biases and motives behind this curated list.

Franchisors are naturally motivated to present their business in the best possible light to potential franchisees. By directing you to specific franchisees, they aim to control the narrative and ensure that you hear positive feedback. These selected franchisees may be those who have had particularly successful experiences or those who have agreed to provide favourable testimonials.

The franchisees on the 'pet list' may have been incentivised to speak positively about the franchise. This could be in the form of financial rewards, discounts on fees, or other benefits. While not inherently unethical, it's important to recognise that their perspective might not fully represent the typical franchisee experience.

The existence of a 'pet list' suggests that the franchisor may be attempting to steer the conversation away from potential pitfalls or challenges. By highlighting only the most successful or satisfied franchisees, they might be downplaying common issues such as high operational costs, market saturation, or lack of support. This tactic can be a red flag if not balanced with transparency. It raises questions about what the franchisor might be trying to hide.

- Are there franchisees who have struggled or failed?
- What are the reasons behind their difficulties?

These are critical questions that need answers before making an investment decision.

To gain a comprehensive understanding of the franchise, it's essential to conduct your own research beyond the 'pet list.' Reach out to a diverse range of franchisees, including those not suggested by the franchisor. This can provide a more balanced view of the franchise's strengths and weaknesses.

When speaking with franchisees, ask probing questions about their experiences. Inquire about their initial expectations versus reality, any challenges they've faced, and the level of support received from the franchisor.

Questions about financial performance, workload, and satisfaction can also provide valuable insights.

While the 'pet list' can be a useful starting point, it's crucial to approach it with a critical mindset. Understanding the potential biases and motivations behind it allows you to seek a more comprehensive view of the franchise. By conducting thorough research and speaking with a wide range of franchisees, you can make an informed decision that aligns with your goals and expectations. This proactive approach ensures that you enter the franchise relationship with a clear understanding of what lies ahead.

Red Flag Tactic

In the world of franchising, due diligence is your most powerful tool. When considering a franchise investment, it's essential to look beyond the surface and delve deeper into the realities of the business. One of the tactics that can obscure your perception is the franchisor's 'pet list' of franchisees. This curated list is often presented to potential

franchisees to showcase the best aspects of the franchise, but it may not always provide the full picture. Here's how to navigate this potential pitfall and ensure a well-rounded evaluation of your franchise opportunity.

When a franchisor provides a 'pet list' of franchisees, it's crucial to be aware of the possibility that this list is designed to present the franchise in the best possible light.

These franchisees may have been handpicked because of their exceptional success or willingness to offer glowing testimonials. While their experiences are valuable, they might not reflect the average franchisee's journey. Look for signs of bias, such as uniformly positive feedback without mention of any challenges or areas for improvement.

Broadening Your Outreach:

To gain a comprehensive understanding of the franchise, it's important to reach out to a wider array of franchisees beyond those recommended by the franchisor. Seek out franchisees who have been in the system for varying lengths of time and those from different regions. This diversity can provide a more balanced view of the franchise's strengths and weaknesses. Online forums, franchisee associations, and industry events can be excellent resources for connecting with a broader network of franchisees.

Conducting Independent Research:

Independent research is a cornerstone of effective due diligence. While the franchisor's information is a starting point, it's essential to verify and supplement it with external sources. Investigate the franchise's reputation within the industry, review financial disclosures, and consult third-party evaluations. This independent research will help you form a more objective assessment of the franchise opportunity.

Understanding Biases and Limitations:

Recognise that the information provided by the franchisor's preferred franchisees may come with biases and limitations. These franchisees might have received incentives for their positive feedback, or they could be experiencing unique circumstances that don't apply to the broader franchise network. Approach their testimonials with a critical mindset, considering both what is said and what might be left unsaid.

Asking the Right Questions:

When speaking with current franchisees, it's crucial to ask insightful questions that elicit honest feedback.

Inquire about their initial expectations versus their actual experiences, any challenges they've faced, and the level of support they receive from the franchisor. Ask about their financial performance, workload, and overall satisfaction. These questions can provide valuable insights into the day- to-day realities of operating the franchise.

Recognising Red Flag Responses:

Be vigilant for 'red flag' responses from franchisees that might indicate underlying issues within the franchise system. Hesitation, vague answers, or reluctance to discuss certain topics can be warning signs. Pay attention to any patterns in the feedback that suggest common challenges or dissatisfaction among franchisees.

Balancing the 'Pet List' with Other Sources:

The 'pet list' is just one piece of the puzzle in the franchise discovery process. While it can offer useful insights,

it's essential to balance this information with other sources. Consider the franchisor's financial performance, market position, and overall reputation. By integrating multiple perspectives, you can develop a well-rounded understanding of the franchise opportunity.

Navigating the franchisor's 'pet list' requires a good eye and a commitment to do thorough research. By broadening your outreach, conducting independent investigations, and asking the right questions, you can uncover the true potential of the franchise and make an informed investment decision. This proactive approach will empower you to enter the franchise relationship with confidence and clarity.

You Should Be Allowed To Speak To Any Franchisee

In the pursuit of a comprehensive understanding of a franchise, being able to speak to the entire franchise network can be invaluable. This approach allows you to gather insights from various perspectives, offering a holistic view of the franchise's operations. By engaging with a wide array of franchisees, you can better assess the consistency of support and success across the network.

This broad engagement is crucial in identifying any recurring issues or challenges that may not be immediately apparent from the franchisor's curated narratives.

Speaking to multiple franchisees also serves as a litmus test for the franchisor's transparency and openness, which can be indicative of their overall business practices. A franchisor willing to facilitate or encourage communication with a broad spectrum of their franchise network often signals a commitment to honesty and integrity. This openness allows potential franchisees to gather a range of insights that can significantly inform their decision-making process.

Speaking with a diverse group of franchisees helps verify the accuracy of the franchisor's claims regarding franchisee satisfaction and profitability. It ensures that the success stories and satisfaction levels are not isolated incidents but rather reflective of the network as a whole.

However, it's important to note that not all franchisees may have given permission for their details to be shared, due to GDPR regulations. In such cases, the franchisor isn't legally allowed to provide their contact information.

Despite this limitation, striving to communicate with as many franchisees as possible remains a critical step in making an informed investment decision. By doing so, you equip yourself with a comprehensive understanding of the franchise landscape, preparing you for a successful venture.

Community Connection

In the world of franchising, the importance of community connection cannot be overstated. Let me share the story of Jane, a prospective franchisee who found herself at a crossroads when deciding whether to invest in a franchise. Jane was drawn to a particular franchise because of its stellar reputation and success stories, but she wanted to ensure she was making an informed decision.

Determined to go beyond the surface, Jane set out to connect with the wider franchisee community. She knew that genuine franchisee testimonials were key to understanding the true nature of the franchise. Rather than solely relying on the franchisor's recommended contacts, she reached out to franchisees through online forums and local business groups. This approach allowed her to hear unfiltered experiences, both positive and negative.

Through these conversations, Jane discovered the critical role of franchisee satisfaction in her decision- making process. She learned about the consistent support provided by the franchisor, which was a major factor in the franchisees' success. The testimonials she gathered painted a picture of a supportive network where franchisees felt valued and heard.

Jane also picked up valuable tips for engaging with the wider franchisee community. She found that approaching franchisees with genuine curiosity and respect opened doors to candid discussions. She asked about their day-to- day operations, challenges, and the support they received from the franchisor. This dialogue not only helped her make a well-rounded decision but also laid the foundation for future connections within the franchise community.

Ultimately, Jane's efforts highlighted the impact of community connection on franchise success. By fostering relationships with other franchisees from the discovery stage, she was able to build a support network that would prove invaluable as she embarked on her own franchising journey. This sense of community provided her with insights, encouragement, and a sense of belonging that went beyond financial metrics.

Jane's story underscores the power of community connection in franchising. It illustrates how engaging with a diverse group of franchisees can enrich your understanding and enhance your chances of success. Her journey reminds us that, in franchising, the relationships you build are just as important as the business itself.

SECRET 4: Cost Of Franchise Agreement Renewal

Renewal Fees Explained

When entering a franchise agreement, the focus is often on the initial investment and the excitement of starting a new business. However, it's equally important to consider the long-term financial commitments, particularly the costs associated with renewing your franchise contract. These renewal fees can be substantial and, if not anticipated, could place a significant financial burden on your business.

One of the most surprising aspects of franchise renewals is the requirement by some franchisors to pay the full initial franchise fee again. This can be perplexing for franchisees who have already invested significant resources to establish and grow their business. The rationale behind this fee is often tied to the franchisor's need to maintain consistent revenue streams and ensure ongoing support and brand development.

However, from a franchisee's perspective, this can feel unjust, especially when you've already proven your capability to run the business successfully. It's crucial to clarify whether this fee applies before signing the initial contract, as it can significantly impact your long-term financial planning.

In addition to the full renewal fee, most franchisors impose a percentage fee based on the turnover of your business. This fee can be particularly burdensome, as it effectively reduces your profit margin. In some cases, these fees can exceed 30% of your annual turnover, which can be a substantial financial drain. The justification for these fees often lies in the continued use of the franchisor's brand, systems, and support. However, it's important to weigh these costs against the benefits you're receiving.

Are the franchisor's contributions still adding significant value to your business? Understanding this balance is key to determining whether the renewal terms are fair and sustainable.

Beyond the renewal and percentage fees, legal fees associated with the renewal process can also add up. Franchisors may charge for the administrative and legal aspects of renewing the contract and work required to renew your contract. While these fees might seem minor compared to the other costs, they can still amount to thousands of pounds. It's essential to have a clear understanding of what these legal fees cover and whether they are negotiable. Some franchisors might be open to reducing or waiving these fees, especially if you have demonstrated strong performance and loyalty to the brand.

The culmination of these fees can feel like an unfair imposition, especially when considering that they are necessary just to continue operating the business you've worked hard to build. This underscores the importance of thoroughly understanding renewal terms before entering into a franchise agreement.

To avoid financial surprises, it's critical to discuss renewal terms with the franchisor upfront. Ask for detailed information about all potential fees and their justifications.

This knowledge empowers you to make informed decisions and plan effectively for the future. By understanding the full scope of renewal costs, you can ensure that your franchise remains a viable and profitable venture long after the initial excitement has passed.

Hidden Renewal Charges

When entering into a franchise agreement, the excitement of launching a new business can sometimes overshadow the finer details, particularly those related to contract renewals. Hidden renewal charges are a significant factor that can affect your bottom line, and understanding them is crucial for long-term success.

Commonly overlooked renewal fees can include charges for continued use of the brand, systems, and ongoing support. These fees might seem minor initially but can add up over time, impacting your profitability. It's essential to scrutinise the franchise agreement for any clauses related to renewal fees and understand how they can affect your financial planning.

Negotiating better terms before signing the initial franchise agreement is a proactive strategy to mitigate the impact of these charges. Engage in open discussions with the franchisor about potential renewal fees and express any concerns you might have. Some franchisors may be willing to negotiate terms, especially if you demonstrate a strong commitment to the brand and a clear business plan.

Budgeting for renewal costs throughout the franchise term is another critical step in avoiding financial surprises. By setting aside funds regularly, you can ensure that you are prepared for these expenses when they arise. This foresight not only safeguards your business's financial health but also allows you to focus on growth and development without the looming worry of unexpected costs.

Renewal fees can significantly impact long-term business planning and profitability. They can affect cash flow, investment in new opportunities, and even your ability to expand. It's vital to factor these costs into your business model from the outset, ensuring that your franchise remains a sustainable and profitable venture.

Understanding the legal aspects of franchise renewals is essential in protecting your interests. Familiarise yourself with the terms outlined in the franchise agreement and consult with a legal professional if necessary. This knowledge empowers you to navigate the renewal process confidently and ensures that your rights and investments are safeguarded.

By addressing hidden renewal charges head-on, you can make informed decisions that align with your business goals. This proactive approach not only protects your bottom line but also positions your franchise for long-term success.

As a franchisee, it's crucial to take a proactive approach to understanding the financial implications of your franchise agreement. Begin by reviewing your franchise agreement thoroughly, paying close attention to any clauses related to renewal fees.

- Are these fees clearly outlined, and do you understand their potential impact on your business?

- How might these fees affect your cash flow and financial planning over the years?

Once you've identified these clauses, take the time to calculate the long-term cost of these renewal fees on your overall profitability.

By addressing these questions now, you can better prepare for future financial obligations and ensure your business remains on a path to sustained success.

Franchise renewal fees are an important consideration for franchisees as their initial agreement terms come to an end.

Here are some key statistics and figures regarding franchise renewal costs:

Renewal Fee Structures

- Franchise renewal fees can take several forms: A percentage of the current initial franchise fee, the full amount of the current initial franchise fee, a reduced flat fee or no fee at all

Typical Renewal Fee Amounts

- According to industry data: Renewal fees typically range from 1% to 10% of annual sales. Some franchises charge a flat renewal fee, which can vary widely depending

on the brand.34.5% of franchises do not charge any renewal fee at all.

Renewal Fee Timing

- Franchise agreements typically last 10-20 years before renewal is required. At the end of this initial term, franchisees must pay the renewal fee to continue operating under the brand.

Factors Affecting Renewal Costs

- The specific renewal fee amount can depend on factors like: The franchise brand's popularity and success. Length of the franchisee's relationship with the company. The franchisee's performance and compliance record. Current market conditions

Source: https://www.franchiseinfo.co.uk/advice/ introduction-to-franchising/the-true-cost-of-running-a- franchise-infographic/

The Renewal Realisation

When Mario came to me with his story, it was a stark reminder of the importance of fully understanding franchise renewal terms before committing to an agreement. Mario, an experienced franchisee who had previously owned another franchise, found himself blind- sided by the renewal terms of his current franchise.

He hadn't fully comprehended the scope, scale, or viability of these terms when he first signed on. The requirement to pay 25% of his annual turnover as a renewal fee - on top of the existing royalty fees - was staggering. To me, this seemed like sheer greed, and I struggle to find any justification for such an exorbitant demand.

The real issue for Mario was that his business was generating a significant turnover, but he didn't have the cash on hand to cover this unexpected expense. He was forced to seek financing just to meet the renewal fee, which put additional strain on his business. The alternative was even more daunting: relinquishing his business back to the franchisor, who would likely sell it to someone else. It's hard not to suspect an ulterior motive here, as the franchisor stood to gain either way.

Mario's experience serves as a cautionary tale for anyone considering a franchise investment. It underscores the critical need to thoroughly review and understand renewal terms, ensuring they are fair and sustainable. It's a reminder that while franchising can be a pathway to success, it's essential to navigate it with eyes wide open, armed with knowledge and a clear understanding of all the financial commitments involved.

SECRET 5: Monthly Fees & Charges

Types Of Monthly Fees

When entering a franchise agreement, it's essential to consider not just the initial investment but also the

ongoing monthly fees that are part and parcel of operating a franchise. These fees are critical to maintaining the franchisor-franchisee relationship and ensuring the continuous support and development of the brand.

However, they can also significantly impact your bottom line, making it crucial to understand their structure and implications.

Royalty Fees:

Royalty fees are a staple in the franchise industry, typically calculated as a percentage of your monthly turnover. These fees are the primary source of income for franchisors, allowing them to provide ongoing support, brand development, and operational guidance. The standard range for these fees is between 10% and 12% of your monthly revenue (+VAT), but this can vary depending on the franchise.

While these fees contribute to the franchisor's ability to maintain and enhance the brand, they can also pose a challenge for franchisees, especially during periods of low revenue. It's essential to factor these fees into your financial planning from the outset, ensuring that your business model can sustain them without compromising profitability.

Minimum Monthly Fee:

In addition to percentage-based royalty fees, many franchisors impose a minimum monthly fee. This ensures that the franchisor receives a baseline income, regardless of your business's performance. For franchisees, this means that even during slow months, you are obligated to pay a set amount, which can be around £350 (+VAT) or more.

This minimum fee acts as a safety net for franchisors, but for franchisees, it underscores the importance of maintaining consistent sales levels. If your business is consistently paying the minimum fee, it may indicate a need to reassess your strategies or seek additional support from the franchisor to boost sales.

Marketing Levy:

Another common component of monthly fees is the marketing levy. This fee is pooled with contributions from other franchisees and used to fund national or regional marketing campaigns. The idea is to enhance brand visibility and attract more customers, benefiting all franchisees collectively.

While this can relieve some of the marketing burden from individual franchisees, it's important to understand how these funds are allocated. Not all marketing efforts may directly benefit your specific location, so it's worth discussing with the franchisor how these campaigns are planned and executed. Transparency in marketing strategies can help you assess whether the levy is providing value to your business.

Monthly fees are an integral part of the franchising model, supporting the infrastructure that allows franchisees to thrive. However, they also represent a significant financial commitment that can impact your profitability. Understanding the structure and purpose of these fees is

crucial for effective financial planning.

To navigate monthly fees successfully, it's important to have a clear understanding of what each fee covers and how it benefits your business. Engage in open discussions with the franchisor about fee structures, potential increases, and the support you can expect in return. By doing so, you ensure that these fees contribute positively to your business's growth and sustainability, allowing you to focus on building a successful franchise.

Why Do Franchisors Charge Royalty Payments?

Franchise royalty payments are a common and fundamental component of the franchising business model, representing the ongoing fees that a franchisee pays to the franchisor. These payments are typically calculated as a percentage of the franchisee's sales or revenue, reflecting the franchise's performance and success. The specific terms, including the rate and frequency of royalty payments, are meticulously outlined in the franchise agreement, providing a clear framework for both parties involved.

The essence of royalty fees lies in their role as compensation for the franchisor. They cover the continued use of the brand, along with the support and resources that the franchisor provides to the franchisee. This includes access to established business systems, training, marketing support, and operational guidance, all of which are crucial for maintaining the franchise's standards and success.

Royalty payments are not merely a financial obligation but a critical aspect of the franchising business model. They ensure the franchisor's financial sustainability, enabling them to invest in brand development, innovation, and the overall support of the franchise network. This ongoing financial contribution from franchisees allows the franchisor to maintain a robust infrastructure that benefits all parties involved, fostering a thriving and cohesive franchise community.

Understanding the nature and purpose of franchise royalty payments is essential for anyone considering entering a franchise agreement. It highlights the symbiotic relationship between the franchisor and franchisee, where both parties contribute to and benefit from the brand's success. By appreciating the role of royalty payments, franchisees can better navigate their financial commitments and ensure that they are leveraging the full range of support and resources available to them, ultimately driving their business towards success.

Franchise royalty payments in the UK typically range from 4% to 12% of the franchisee's gross revenue, aligning with the standard practices observed globally. This range ensures that franchisees contribute a fair share to the franchisor, which in turn supports the brand's ongoing development and the provision of essential resources and support.

The specific percentage of royalty fees can vary significantly depending on the industry. For instance, franchises in sectors with higher sales volumes, such as fast food, often have lower royalty percentages. This is because their substantial revenue streams can sustain the franchisor's needs even at a reduced rate. Conversely, franchises with lower annual revenues might face higher royalty percentages to compensate for the smaller revenue base and ensure the franchisor receives adequate support.

To illustrate, consider a fast-food franchise in the UK earning £2 million in annual revenue with a 5% royalty fee. This franchise would contribute £100,000 annually in royalties. Meanwhile, a consultancy firm generating £400,000 annually with a 10% royalty fee would pay £40,000 in royalties.

These examples highlight how the royalty fee structure is designed to align with the revenue potential of different industries.

Royalty fees are typically paid on a regular schedule, such as weekly, monthly, or quarterly, with the specific frequency detailed in the franchise agreement. This regularity ensures a steady flow of income for the franchisor, facilitating consistent support for the franchise network.

In addition to royalty fees, many franchises impose a separate marketing fee, which generally ranges from 1% to 4% of gross revenue. This fee is pooled to fund marketing efforts that enhance brand visibility and attract customers across the franchise network.

Some franchisors implement variable royalty fee structures to incentivise growth and multi-unit expansion. For example:

- Revenue up to £1 million: 6% royalty
- Revenue from £1 million to £2 million: 5.5% royalty
- Revenue over £2 million: 5% royalty

This tiered approach encourages franchisees to increase their revenue, rewarding them with reduced royalty rates as they expand their business.

Royalty fees are a cornerstone of the franchise business model, providing ongoing support and resources to franchisees while serving as the primary income source for franchisors.

Why Do Franchisors Charge A Marketing Levy?

In the franchising world, a marketing levy is a fee that franchisees contribute towards a collective marketing fund. This fund is managed by the franchisor and is used to finance national or regional marketing campaigns aimed at enhancing brand visibility and attracting customers across the franchise network. The primary purpose of a marketing levy is to pool resources for large-scale marketing efforts that individual franchisees might not be able to afford on their own.

Calculation and Coverage: Marketing levies are typically calculated as a percentage of the franchisee's gross revenue. The exact percentage is specified in the franchise agreement and can vary depending on the franchisor's marketing strategy and the industry in which the franchise operates. These funds generally cover advertising campaigns, promotional activities, public relations efforts, and sometimes even digital marketing initiatives designed to benefit the entire franchise network.

Benefits of a Collective Marketing Fund: Contributing to a collective marketing fund offers several advantages. It allows franchisees to benefit from high-impact marketing campaigns that enhance brand recognition and customer acquisition. By pooling resources, franchisees can achieve a level of market penetration and visibility that would

be challenging to accomplish individually. This collective approach also ensures consistency in branding and messaging, which is crucial for maintaining the integrity of the franchise's image.

Considerations and Potential Drawbacks: While marketing levies can be beneficial, there are important considerations to keep in mind. One potential drawback is that not all marketing efforts may directly benefit every franchise location, which can lead to concerns about the return

on investment for individual franchisees. Additionally, some franchisors may use marketing levies as a means to generate revenue for themselves rather than strictly for marketing purposes. Since marketing levies are not regulated, there is no legal obligation for franchisors to spend the entire levy on marketing activities. This lack of regulation can sometimes lead to a lack of transparency in how the funds are allocated.

For franchisees, it's crucial to engage in open discussions with the franchisor about how marketing levies are used and to seek transparency in the allocation of these funds. If in doubt, ask for proof!

What Are Franchise Management Fees?

Franchise management fees, are ongoing payments that franchisees make to franchisors as part of their franchise agreement. These fees are a crucial component of the franchising model, ensuring the sustainability and quality of the franchise network.

Purpose of Management Fees:

The primary purpose of franchise management fees is to reimburse the franchisor for providing ongoing support and services to franchisees. These fees cover a wide range of activities, including the use of the brand name, marketing efforts, operational support, and ongoing training. Additionally, management fees help finance the monitoring of franchisee performance, conducting market research, and the continuous development of the franchise system. For the franchisor, these fees also serve as a source of profit, enabling them to invest in brand growth and maintain high standards across the network.

Franchise management fees are usually structured in one of two ways: as a percentage of the franchisee's sales revenue or as a fixed monthly fee. The percentage-based approach is the most common, aligning the fee with the success of the franchisee's business. This method ensures that the franchisor's income grows in tandem with the franchisee's revenue. Alternatively, some franchisors may opt for a fixed monthly fee, which can range from hundreds to thousands of pounds, depending on the franchise system.

Several factors can influence the amount of management fees. These include the level of support and services provided by the franchisor, industry standards for similar franchise concepts, and the overall financial model and profitability of the franchise system. The specific terms and percentages are outlined in the franchise agreement, providing clarity and transparency for both parties.

When evaluating franchise opportunities, potential franchisees should carefully review how management fees are calculated and what they cover. It's important to consider the fee amount in relation to projected revenues and profits, ensuring that the financial model is sustainable. Franchisees should also understand that lower fees don't necessarily equate to better value if the support and resources provided are lacking.

Franchise management fees are an essential part of the ongoing financial relationship between franchisors and franchisees. They help fund the support and development of the franchise system while providing a revenue stream for the franchisor. By understanding the structure and purpose of these fees, franchisees can make informed decisions and ensure they receive the necessary support to thrive within the franchise network.

It's important to be aware that some franchisors may charge both a royalty fee and a separate management fee. This dual fee structure can significantly impact the overall financial obligations of a franchisee. While royalty fees are typically a percentage of gross sales and cover the use of the brand and ongoing support, management fees might be additional charges for specific services or operational support.

Before entering into a franchise agreement, it's crucial to thoroughly review the fee structure and understand what each fee covers. Ensure that the combined cost of these fees aligns with the value and support provided by the franchisor.

This understanding will help you assess the overall financial viability of the franchise opportunity and avoid unexpected financial burdens.

SECRET 6: The Claims About Franchise Training

The Training Claims

Franchising often comes with the promise of comprehensive training, with many franchisors claiming that they can train anyone to succeed in their business model. While training is undoubtedly a crucial element of franchising, it's important to recognise that not every franchise is suitable for every individual.

Success in franchising requires more than just training; it requires a good match between your skills and the demands of the business. Franchisors typically provide training programmes designed to equip new franchisees with the knowledge and skills needed to operate the business effectively. These programmes can cover a wide range of topics, from operational procedures and customer service to marketing strategies and financial management. The promise of training can be reassuring, especially for those entering a new industry. However, it's essential to approach these promises with a critical eye.

While training can provide a solid foundation, it cannot transform someone into an expert overnight, especially if the business requires skills that are vastly different from your own. When considering a franchise, it's crucial to assess whether your skills and interests align with the business's requirements. For instance, if you're looking at a retail or food franchise, consider whether you have the aptitude for managing a large team. These businesses often require strong leadership, organisational skills, and the ability to handle high-pressure situations. If managing staff isn't your forte, you might find yourself overwhelmed, regardless of the training provided.

Similarly, if you're considering a tech franchise but lack proficiency with computers, you may struggle to keep up with the technical demands, even with extensive training. It's important to be honest about your strengths and weaknesses and choose a franchise that complements your skill set. Training is designed to enhance your existing skills and provide you with the tools needed to succeed. It can fill knowledge gaps, introduce you to the franchisor's systems, and teach you industry-specific best practices. However, it cannot replace the innate abilities or interests that make you well-suited for a particular type of business.

Before committing to a franchise, evaluate whether the training offered will genuinely prepare you for the challenges ahead. Ask detailed questions about the training programme's content, duration, and delivery method. Consider whether it addresses areas where you feel less confident and how it supports ongoing learning and development. Choosing a franchise that doesn't align with your skills can lead to frustration and potential failure. Not only might the business struggle, but you could also find yourself responsible for ongoing fees until the franchise is resold. This underscores the importance of selecting a franchise that fits your personal and professional profile.

While franchisors may claim they can train anyone, the reality is that success in franchising hinges on a good match between your skills and the business model. Take the time to assess your abilities and interests, and choose a franchise that aligns with them. By doing so, you increase your chances of thriving in the franchise world, supported by training that enhances your strengths and prepares you for success.

Invest In A Franchise That Suits Your Skills

When considering a franchise, it's essential to focus on finding one that aligns with your unique skill set. Assessing your skills is the first step in this journey. Understanding your strengths and weaknesses can help you identify which franchise opportunities are most compatible with your abilities. This introspection is crucial, as it allows you to match your skills to the specific requirements of a franchise. A perfect alignment can enhance your chances of success, as your existing skills will complement the training and operational demands of the business.

Passion also plays a significant role in your franchise choice. When you are passionate about the business, you're more likely to invest the time and energy needed to make it succeed. Passion fuels perseverance, especially when faced with challenges. It's important to choose a franchise that not only matches your skills but also ignites your enthusiasm.

Understanding the training provided by the franchisor is another critical aspect. Evaluate the depth and quality of the training program. Does it cover all necessary areas, from operational procedures to customer service and marketing strategies? A comprehensive training program should equip you with the knowledge and skills needed to manage the business effectively. However, it's important to set realistic expectations.

Training programs can provide a solid foundation but may not turn you into an expert overnight.

Ongoing support and training are vital components of a successful franchise operation. Continuous learning opportunities can help you adapt to changing market conditions and refine your skills. Look for franchisors who offer robust support systems and encourage ongoing professional development.

Consider case studies of successful franchisees whose skills aligned well with the training provided. These stories can offer valuable insights into how the right match between skills and training can lead to success. Conversely, be aware of red flags that might suggest a need to reconsider your franchise choice. If the training seems inadequate or misaligned with your skill set, it might be wise to explore other options.

As you prepare to maximise franchise training opportunities, take proactive steps to align your skills with the business requirements. Seek additional resources or training if necessary, and approach the franchisor with questions about how their program can support your growth. By doing so, you position yourself to make the most of the training provided and set a strong foundation for your franchise journey.

By carefully assessing your skills, aligning them with the right franchise, and fully engaging with the training and support offered, you can enhance your chances of thriving in the franchise world. This thoughtful approach ensures that you are well-prepared to face the challenges and enjoy the rewards of franchising.

The Franchise Team

The support provided by the franchisor is a cornerstone of success. A robust franchise team offers invaluable expertise, guiding you through the complexities of running your business. This team typically comprises industry experts, trainers, and support staff who are dedicated to ensuring your success. They provide comprehensive training programs that delve into the nuances of the business model, equipping you with the tools needed to navigate the operational landscape effectively.

The true depth and quality of these training programs are pivotal. They must align with the practical demands of running the franchise, addressing everything from daily operations to customer service and marketing strategies. A well-structured training program ensures that you're not only prepared to manage the business but also to excel in it. The alignment of training with real-world demands is crucial for translating theoretical knowledge into practical skills.

Beyond initial training, ongoing support from the franchise team is essential. This support includes regular check-ins, additional training sessions, and access to resources that help you adapt to market changes. Continuous support ensures that you remain aligned with the franchise's standards and can tackle any challenges that arise. Real- life examples abound of franchisees who have thrived thanks to the robust training and support provided by their franchisors. These success stories highlight the transformative impact that quality training and ongoing support can have on your business.

The franchise team also plays a vital role in ensuring compliance and brand consistency. They provide guidelines and frameworks that help you adhere to the franchise's standards, safeguarding the brand's reputation. This oversight is crucial for maintaining the quality and integrity of the franchise across all locations.

As a franchisee, you may also need to build your own team to support your business operations. Depending on the franchise model, this might include hiring staff for customer service, operations, and marketing. Your team should complement the support provided by the franchisor, ensuring that your business runs smoothly and efficiently.

To maximise the value of training for long-term business growth, it's important to engage actively with the resources provided. Take advantage of every opportunity for learning and development, and implement the strategies and best practices shared by the franchise team. By doing so, you can drive growth and ensure the sustained success of your franchise.

With support from the franchise team, combined with your own efforts it creates a robust foundation for success. By leveraging the expertise and resources provided, you can navigate the challenges of franchising with confidence and achieve your business goals.

SECRET 7: The Hidden Operations Manual

Always See The Operations Manual

When you invest in a franchise, one of the key components you pay for is access to the franchisor's training and operations manual. This document is more than just a guide; it's a comprehensive blueprint that encapsulates the franchisor's accumulated expertise, operational strategies, and best practices. Understanding its significance and ensuring its quality is paramount to your success as a franchisee.

The training manual serves as an essential resource for franchisees, providing detailed instructions on how to operate the business effectively. It covers a wide range of areas, including daily operations, customer service protocols, marketing strategies, financial management, and compliance with brand standards. Essentially, it is designed to ensure that every franchisee can replicate the franchisor's proven business model consistently.

Before signing a franchise agreement, it's vital to request access to the training manual. This allows you to evaluate its quality and assess whether it meets your needs. A comprehensive and well-organised manual indicates that the franchisor is committed to your success and has invested in creating a robust support system.

If a franchisor is reluctant to share the manual before you've signed the contract, consider it a red flag.

Transparency is key in a successful franchisor-franchisee relationship, and access to the manual should be part of your due diligence process.

When reviewing the training manual, look for clarity, structure, and professionalism. A well-crafted manual should be easy to navigate, with clear headings, indexed sections, and concise instructions. It should cover all aspects of the business comprehensively, leaving no room for ambiguity. A poorly structured or confusing manual can hinder your ability to run the business effectively. It may indicate that the franchisor has not fully developed their operational processes or that they lack the commitment to providing adequate support.

The training manual should be practical and actionable, serving as a day-to-day reference tool. It should help you troubleshoot common issues, streamline operations, and maintain consistency with the brand's standards. This resource is crucial, especially during the initial stages of your franchise journey, when you are still learning the ropes.

Discovering that the training manual is of little practical use after signing the agreement can be detrimental. It can lead to operational inefficiencies, increased stress, and potential financial losses. Ensuring the manual's quality beforehand can prevent these challenges and set you up for a smoother transition into franchise ownership.

Assess The Content Of The Manual

Assessing the content of a franchise's operations manual is a crucial step in determining the potential success of your franchise venture. A comprehensive operations manual is not just a procedural guide; it is the backbone of your business operations, encapsulating the franchisor's knowledge and best practices. Its importance cannot be overstated, as it serves as a critical resource for ensuring

consistency and efficiency in your franchise.

When evaluating an operations manual, there are key sections you should look for. These include detailed instructions on daily operations, customer service protocols, marketing strategies, financial management, and compliance with brand standards. Each section should provide clear and actionable guidance, enabling you to replicate the franchisor's successful business model.

The clarity and detail of the manual's instructions are paramount. A well-structured manual should be easy to navigate, with clear headings, indexed sections, and concise instructions. It should leave no room for ambiguity, providing you with the confidence to manage your franchise effectively.

The role of the operations manual in daily franchise management is significant; it should be a go-to resource for troubleshooting issues, streamlining operations, and maintaining brand consistency.

However, not all manuals are created equal. Red flags in operations manuals can include vague instructions, outdated information, or a lack of comprehensive coverage. These issues can hinder your ability to run the business effectively and may indicate a lack of commitment from the franchisor. Comparing manuals across different franchises can provide valuable insights into the level of support and detail you can expect.

An inadequate operations manual can have a detrimental impact on franchise success. It can lead to operational inefficiencies, increased stress, and potential financial losses. Therefore, it's essential to seek clarification and updates on manual content when necessary. A proactive approach to understanding the manual ensures you are well-prepared for the challenges of franchise ownership.

Ultimately, the operations manual is a reflection of the franchisor's support and commitment. A comprehensive, clear, and detailed manual signifies that the franchisor is invested in your success and has developed a robust support system to help you thrive. By thoroughly assessing the content of the manual, you can make an informed decision about whether a franchise is the right fit for you, setting the stage for a successful business journey.

Be Very Wary If They Are Reluctant To Share

Transparency is a cornerstone of successful franchisor-franchisee relationships. When a franchisor is open and willing to share operational details, it builds trust and sets a strong foundation for collaboration. However, reluctance to share such information can be a significant red flag. It may indicate that the franchisor is withholding critical details that could impact your ability to manage the franchise effectively.

Entering a franchise agreement without full disclosure can have serious consequences. Without access to comprehensive operational information, you may find yourself unprepared for the realities of running the business. This lack of transparency can lead to unexpected challenges, operational inefficiencies, and potential financial losses. It's essential to ensure that you have all the necessary information to make an informed decision before committing to a franchise.

To safeguard yourself, adopt strategies that ensure access to all required operational information. Request to review the operations manual and other relevant documents before signing any agreements.

Ask detailed questions about the business model, daily operations, and support systems. A franchisor who is committed to your success will be forthcoming with this information.

BIG WARNING: If you don't see the manual or if the franchisor is evasive about sharing it, be cautious. There may be requirements or obligations within the franchise that you are not comfortable with or prepared to handle. This lack of visibility could lead to situations where you're expected to perform tasks or adhere to practices that don't align with your skills or values.

Transparency is crucial in evaluating a franchise opportunity. Ensure that you have full access to all operational details and that the franchisor is open to sharing this information. By doing so, you protect yourself from unforeseen challenges and set the stage for a successful and mutually beneficial franchise relationship.

The Conclusion To These 7 Dirty Secrets

In conclusion, while franchising offers a structured path to business ownership, it is not without its complexities and challenges. As we've revealed through the seven dirty secrets, understanding these intricacies is crucial for aspiring franchisees.

Alongside these insights, several key considerations can further guide your franchising journey.

Selecting the right location and understanding the demographics of your target area are paramount. The success of a franchise often hinges on its accessibility and the local demand for its offerings. Conduct thorough market research to ensure your chosen location aligns with your business goals and customer base.

Ongoing support and training beyond the initial setup are vital for sustaining growth and adapting to market changes. A franchise that invests in continuous development and provides a robust support network can significantly enhance your operational success.

Financial performance is another critical area, with profit margins and break-even points varying across franchises.

Understanding these metrics can help you set realistic expectations and develop strategies to achieve profitability.

Effective marketing and customer acquisition strategies tailored to franchising can further boost your business.

Leverage both traditional and digital channels to reach your audience, and focus on building strong customer relationships.

Innovation and adaptation play a crucial role in the long- term success of a franchise. In today's rapidly changing market, the ability to evolve and embrace new trends can set your franchise apart from competitors.

Legal considerations are also essential, and engaging a franchise attorney to review agreements can protect your interests and ensure compliance with all legal obligations.

Transitioning from an employee to a franchise owner requires a shift in mindset. Prepare yourself psychologically for the challenges of entrepreneurship by building resilience and seeking mentorship from experienced franchisees.

Examining case studies of both successful and unsuccessful franchises can provide valuable lessons. Understanding what works and what doesn't can help you navigate potential pitfalls and replicate successful strategies.

Finally, if you ever consider selling your franchise, understanding the resale process, including valuation and finding buyers, is crucial for maximising your return on investment.

By arming yourself with knowledge and approaching franchising with a strategic mindset, you can overcome these challenges and build a thriving business. Remember, success in franchising lies in thorough preparation, continuous learning, and the ability to adapt to an ever- evolving landscape.

Franchises Are 5 Times More Likely To Succeed

Proven Formulas And High Success Rates

Despite the challenges, franchising remains an extraordinary pathway into business ownership. It offers the advantage of a tried-and-tested business model, reducing the risks associated with starting a new venture. The support of a franchisor provides a safety net, offering training, marketing, and operational guidance that can accelerate your journey to success.

Franchising also allows you to leverage the power of an established brand, benefiting from its reputation and customer base. This can lead to quicker market entry and increased customer trust, both of which are invaluable for new business owners.

Moreover, franchising offers a structured environment with clear guidelines and support systems, making it an excellent choice for those who thrive in organised settings. It provides the opportunity to learn from industry experts and connect with a network of fellow franchisees, fostering a community of shared knowledge and support.

While it's essential to be aware of the potential pitfalls, franchising can be a powerful vehicle for achieving your entrepreneurial dreams. By conducting thorough research, understanding the intricacies of the franchise agreement, and choosing a franchise that aligns with your skills and goals, you can embark on a fulfilling and prosperous business journey.

FACT: FRANCHISES ARE 5 TIMES MORE LIKELY TO SUCCEED THAN A START-UP BUSINESS

As we've explored the complexities and potential pitfalls within the franchising world, it's essential to find a franchise that not only meets your business aspirations but also aligns with your values.

What to Look For in a Franchise

1.   Ethical, Honest, and Transparent Practices: Look for a franchise that places integrity at the heart of its operations. Transparency and honesty in franchise agreements are crucial for building trust. Ensure that the terms and conditions are upfront and fair, allowing you to feel confident in your investment and partnership.

2.   Proven Success and Comprehensive Support: Seek out franchises with a strong track record and a network

of successful franchisees. Comprehensive training programmes, ongoing support, and marketing resources are vital to equipping you with the tools you need to thrive. A supportive community where you can learn, grow, and share experiences with fellow franchisees is invaluable.

3.   Alignment with Your Values and Goals: Choose a franchise that resonates with your personal and professional values. It's important that the franchise aligns with your skills and long-term goals to ensure a fulfilling and prosperous business journey.

The Unseen Benefits Of Being In a Franchise

One of the significant yet often unseen benefits of joining a franchise is the immediate brand recognition it offers. This provides a substantial head start in market penetration, as customers are more likely to trust a known entity.

- Market Trust: Customers are naturally inclined to trust established brands, reducing the effort needed to build credibility.
- Faster Market Penetration: With a recognised name, franchisees can enter the market more swiftly and effectively.
- Competitive Edge: Leveraging an established brand helps differentiate from local competitors and can lead to increased market share.

The power of an established brand can significantly ease the challenges of gaining customer trust and loyalty.

Franchisees also benefit from access to proprietary software, which streamlines operations and allows for efficient management of daily tasks. This technology is often tailored to the specific needs of the franchise, providing tools that can enhance productivity and operational efficiency.

- Operational Efficiency: Tailored software solutions streamline complex processes, saving time and reducing errors.

- Data Management: Centralised systems allow for better tracking of performance metrics, aiding in strategic decision-making.
- Cost Savings: By utilising franchisor-provided software, franchisees avoid the high costs associated with developing or purchasing external solutions.

Ongoing training is another invaluable benefit, ensuring that franchisees remain up-to-date with the latest industry practices and standards.

- Industry Relevance: Regular training sessions ensure franchisees are aware of the latest trends and regulatory changes.
- Skill Enhancement: Continuous learning opportunities help franchisees and their teams develop new skills and improve existing ones.
- Adaptability: Training equips franchisees to swiftly adapt to market changes, ensuring sustained business growth.

This continuous learning environment helps franchisees adapt to changes and maintain a competitive edge in the market.

Moreover, being part of a franchise network means having the opportunity to connect with other franchise owners. This fosters a community of shared knowledge and support, which can lead to collaborative growth and innovation.

- Community Support: A network of peers provides emotional and professional support, reducing the feeling of isolation often experienced by business owners.

- Collaborative Opportunities: Sharing insights and strategies can lead to innovative solutions and collaborative ventures.

- Knowledge Sharing: Franchisees can learn from the successes and challenges of others, gaining valuable insights to apply to their own operations.

Networking within this community not only provides emotional and professional support but also opens doors to new ideas and strategies that can drive success.

In conclusion, the unseen benefits of being part of a franchise extend far beyond the initial allure of brand recognition and established business models. These advantages form a robust framework that supports franchisees in their pursuit of success. From the trust and credibility that a recognised brand brings, to the streamlined operations enabled by proprietary software, franchisees are equipped with the tools necessary for efficient and effective management.

Ongoing training ensures that franchisees remain at the forefront of industry standards and practices, fostering a culture of continuous improvement and adaptability. Furthermore, the opportunity to network with fellow franchise owners creates a vibrant community where collaboration and shared learning lead to innovation and growth.

Together, these benefits create a nurturing environment where franchisees can thrive, transforming potential challenges into opportunities for development. By leveraging these unseen advantages, franchisees can confidently navigate the complexities of business ownership, paving the way for a prosperous and fulfilling entrepreneurial journey.

My Turning Point

Throughout my years of speaking with individuals eager to embark on their entrepreneurial journeys, I've witnessed first-hand the diverse experiences people have had with franchisors.

These interactions have shaped my understanding of what it truly means to deliver value - a principle that is essential for creating long-term, mutually beneficial relationships.

In my conversations, I've encountered a spectrum of emotions.

Yes, there have been arguments and heated discussions, and I've had to navigate some truly challenging and sad situations. However, I've learned that honesty and ethics are not just moral choices - they are fundamental to sustainable success. Being underhanded and dishonest might yield short-term gains, but they rarely pave the way for enduring prosperity.

Many aspiring entrepreneurs reach the inevitable crossroads where they recognise the need for change. This moment is often a critical point of introspection, where the desire to transition from employee to business owner becomes undeniable. In assessing the franchise landscape, it's crucial to identify both opportunities and potential pitfalls. This evaluation aids in making informed decisions that align with personal goals and the franchise's potential.

The moment of decision is pivotal. It's about evaluating whether your personal goals align with the franchise model you're considering. This requires a leap of faith, as committing to the franchise model involves embracing both its challenges and rewards.

Transitioning from an employee to a franchise owner is a significant shift, requiring not only a change in mindset but also the ability to leverage the expertise and resources provided by the franchisor. This support system is invaluable in building a strong foundation for success.

The initial steps in franchise ownership are critical. They involve laying a solid foundation, overcoming early challenges, and developing strategies for adaptation and growth. These efforts are essential in achieving the milestone of breaking even and moving beyond.

Reflecting on my journey and the journeys of those I've guided, I see the profound personal and financial transformations that franchise ownership can bring. It's a path filled with learning, growth, and the satisfaction of building something meaningful and sustainable.

So, as you stand at the crossroads of your entrepreneurial journey, remember that while caution and thorough research are essential, the world of franchising holds incredible potential.

If you're considering this path, take care to choose wisely, aligning your choice with your values and aspirations.

With honesty and integrity as your guiding principles, franchising can indeed be an amazing opportunity. It offers a structured yet flexible framework for success, allowing you to build a rewarding and sustainable business. Embrace the journey with confidence, knowing that with the right franchise, you can achieve your dreams and create a prosperous future.

Sam

The 'QUESTIONS TO ASK' Checklist!

Starting a franchising is a significant commitment, and ensuring you have all the necessary information is crucial to making an informed decision.

This checklist of questions is designed to guide you through an interview with potential franchisors.

By asking these questions, you can uncover vital details about the franchise opportunity, assess the support and resources available, and evaluate whether the franchise aligns with your business goals and values.

Being thorough in your inquiry will help you compare different franchises and choose the one that best suits your needs.

The 33 Questions you need to ask the franchisor before signing anything!

1.   What's the total cost of getting to open the door to customers on day one?

2.   What about any additional costs not included in the figure above?

3.   If I have over a deposit and don't start trading, will I get my money back?

4.   How much working capital does the business require?

5.   How long do I have to make my working capital available for and what happens to any unused money?

6.   How is the working capital figure broken down into categories?

7.   How long is the period between signing for the franchise until trading starts?

8.   What are the details of any training, and how long does it take to complete full training?

9.   Does the franchise fee include all my ongoing training costs, or do I have to make additional contributions?

10.   What is the break-even figure?

11.   How long should I consider trading to reach the projected break-even figure?

12.   What are the ongoing franchise or management fees?

13.   How are any ongoing franchise or management fees calculated?

14.   How much do I have to contribute to the franchise marketing spend?

15.   If so, how much of the franchise marketing spend do I pay, and how is my share calculated?

16.   Who pays for local advertising costs, and are these costs included in my franchise fee?

17.   Do you have franchise sites available?

18.   If so, how many franchisees are available, and what are the locations?

19.   If not, what are the site selection criteria, and is there a prospective franchisee waiting list?

20. Can I have a full list of current franchises and their contact details?

21. Am I free to contact other franchisees at random and ask any questions that I wish?

22. Can I see the franchise management and operating manuals prior to signing a contract?

23. Have any franchises failed, and why?

24. What are the franchisee selection procedures and the success rates compared to applications received?

25. If the franchisor operates in areas with similar demographics to your territory, how are they performing?

26. Can I have a precise map showing the postcodes covered and territory boundaries?

27. What are the grievance procedures between franchisees and the franchisor?

28. Are there plans for any new products and services in the franchise development pipeline?

29. As you are dependent on the success of your franchisees and the percentage of royalties you charge them, can I see your latest accounts and your management accounts to date?

30. Can I take up bank and trade references?

31. Does the franchise impose any operating restrictions?

32. Can the franchisor provide a sample franchise contract?

33. How many hours will you invest to build a viable customer base that meets the break-even point and then goes on to make a reasonable profit?

By asking these comprehensive questions, you are taking proactive steps to safeguard your investment and ensure a successful franchising experience.

The insights you gain from these discussions will empower you to make informed decisions, negotiate terms that meet your expectations, and select a franchise that aligns with your aspirations.

Remember, the more you know upfront, the better prepared you'll be to navigate the challenges and opportunities of franchising.